WHEN △ DISASTER △ STRIKES

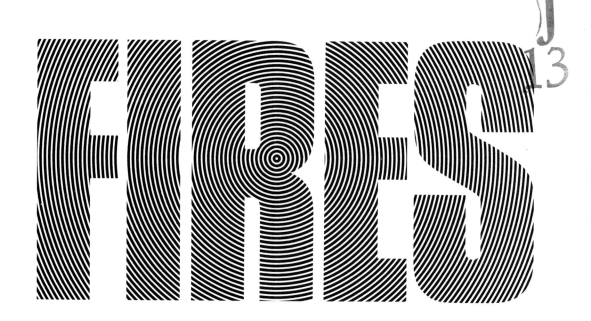

FIRES

J
13

Leigh Wood

TFCB

TWENTY-FIRST CENTURY BOOKS

A Division of Henry Holt and Company
New York

Twenty-First Century Books
A division of Henry Holt and Company, Inc.
115 West 18th Street
New York, New York 10011

Henry Holt® and colophon are trademarks of Henry Holt and
Company, Inc.
Publishers since 1866

©1994 by Blackbirch Graphics, Inc.
First Edition
5   4   3 2   1

Published in Canada by Fitzhenry & Whiteside Ltd.
195 Allstate Parkway, Markham, Ontario L3R 4T8

Printed in the United States of America

All editions are printed on acid-free paper ∞.

Created and produced in association with Blackbirch Graphics, Inc.

Library of Congress Cataloging-in-Publication Data

Wood, Leigh Hope.
    Fires / Leigh Wood. — 1st ed.
        p.   cm. — (When disaster strikes)
    Includes index.
    ISBN 0-8050-3094-8 (alk. paper)
    1. Fires—North America—Juvenile literature. [1. Fires.] I. Title. II. Series.
TH9448.W66   1994
363.37—dc20

                                                                    93-38268
                                                                         CIP
                                                                          AC

Contents

CHAPTER **1**

A Destructive Force

It was the last day that the Ringling Brothers and Barnum & Bailey Circus was in town, and the children of Hartford, Connecticut, were excited about seeing the show. The weather had turned hot and sticky on July 6, 1944. But, despite the temperature, more than 7,000 people made their way to the huge canvas tent known as the "Big Top."

The crowd, mostly children, spilled into the entrance and found seats among the bleachers and chairs that lined the arena. The tent was enormous and thick wooden poles reached from floor to roof, supporting the canvas top.

Opposite:
Fire has the capacity to destroy almost everything in its path. Wilderness areas, suburban neighborhoods, and cities are each vulnerable to the potential dangers of a blaze in specific ways.

Flames consume the Big Top at the Ringling Brothers and Barnum & Bailey Circus in Hartford, Connecticut, in 1944, during the worst circus tragedy in American history.

The roof's canvas material had been water-proofed with a waxy, candle-like substance called paraffin, which had been thinned with gasoline.

The show started. Lions and tigers shot quickly down the aisles through runway chutes. Trainers followed them into a cage. Next, the death-defying Flying Wallendas entered the center ring and took to the high wire.

Suddenly, a fire was spotted on the canvas wall at the tent's entrance. A circus hand tried to put it out with a few buckets of water. But the fire proceeded up to the tent's top, where it met the paraffin. Within minutes, the roof and the support poles were in flames. The wooden poles came crashing to the ground, bringing burning pieces of canvas with them.

The audience panicked and ran for the opening in the tent where they had entered. But it was covered with a huge wall of flames. All the other exits were blocked with circus equipment. Within ten minutes, the flaming tent collapsed, covering all who were left inside.

Firefighters could do very little when they arrived except pull the victims out from underneath the smoldering canvas. Circus performers looked on sadly as the rescue work revealed just how tragic the fire had been. A total of 168 people lost their lives that day, and another 261

Rescue workers survey the ruins of the Hartford circus and search for victims after the fire that sent more than 7,000 spectators running for their lives.

△ 7

suffered serious injuries. One sad-faced clown, the famous Emmett Kelly, sorrowfully stated, "It was the longest afternoon of my life."

The Toll of Fire

Fires often result in lives lost, and property destroyed. The Hartford circus fire was especially sad because a number of the victims were children. Also, several of the deaths could have been prevented if more exits had been available. This precaution is just one of many now taken to help prevent deaths from fire.

Through the years, much has been learned about how to prevent, escape, or fight fire. That knowledge has been put to use by the people who design and construct buildings, by the government officials who write building codes, and by firefighters. Unfortunately, fires are often caused by people acting carelessly.

According to the National Fire Protection Association (NFPA), the leading cause of civilian fire deaths in the United States and Canada is smoking. From 1985 to 1989, blazes started by cigarettes, matches, and lighters, accounted for 33 percent of the fire deaths in Canada and 25 percent in the United States. Other causes included children playing with fire, cooking and heating accidents, hazardous products (like faulty wiring), and arson.

Fires are also started by natural, environmental conditions. In woodland areas—also called wildlands—fires caused by lightning are very common. Each year, lightning sparks about 10,000 forest fires.

Wildland fires usually cause little property damage. About 80 percent of these fires burn no more than 10 acres (4 hectares) of land. But if they do grow large, these fires can cause great destruction to the forest and its wildlife.

Firefighters survey the progress of a giant wildfire in the American Midwest.

△ 9

However, a new forest may arise out of the ashes of a forest fire. The intense heat of a fire can help fertilize soil. While ridding a forest of diseased or dead trees, and other debris on the forest floor, a fire turns soil into a rich mineral ash. Certain wildflowers, such as fireweed and yarrow, appear from the ash almost immediately. Grass and other plants begin growing, and small animals live off the new growth. Also, certain trees actually benefit from fire, because heat opens their cones. This allows the seeds from the cones to fall to the soil and grow into new trees.

The Nature of Fire

Fire is combustion—a process of chemical reactions that give off light and heat. Fire must generate more heat than it gives off in order to keep itself going. It does so by breaking down fuels such as wood, and by releasing heat that spreads the fire to unburned fuels. Oxygen must be present for combustion to take place. It is the element responsible for combining with other elements—such as hydrocarbons—within the fuels. During this process, hydrocarbons are converted from a solid into gas. The gas is ignited, and flames become visible. Heat then reaches the level needed to carry the flames to new fuel.

There are three components required to create and sustain a fire—fuel, oxygen, and heat. These three components are often described as a fire triangle. If one of the three is removed, a fire will go out. In the forest, firefighters usually try to remove fuel from a fire. They create fire lines, bulldozing vegetation down to the soil. When the fire reaches the fire line, it has no more fuel to carry it further. In the city, firefighters try to remove the heat from a fire by dousing the flames with water.

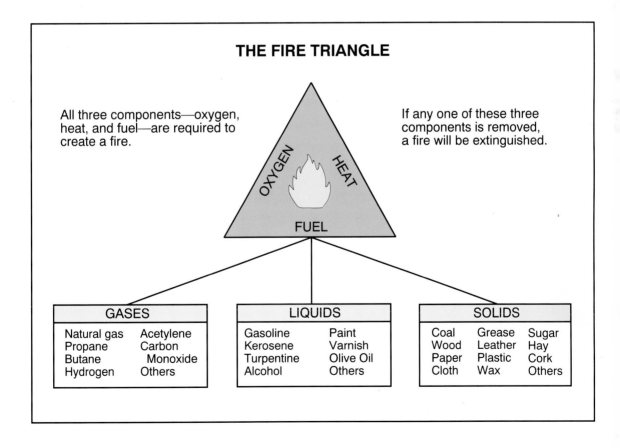

THE FIRE TRIANGLE

All three components—oxygen, heat, and fuel—are required to create a fire.

If any one of these three components is removed, a fire will be extinguished.

OXYGEN   HEAT
FUEL

GASES	
Natural gas	Acetylene
Propane	Carbon
Butane	Monoxide
Hydrogen	Others

LIQUIDS	
Gasoline	Paint
Kerosene	Varnish
Turpentine	Olive Oil
Alcohol	Others

SOLIDS		
Coal	Grease	Sugar
Wood	Leather	Hay
Paper	Plastic	Cork
Cloth	Wax	Others

Fire Is Not All Bad

Fire is not solely a destructive force. In many environments, fire offers the most effective way to break down, or decompose, matter. Fire also helps to recycle nutrients.

The discovery and use of fire is probably one of the single most important events in the history of human evolution. Fire provides heat and light. It also makes cooking possible. And, without fire, there would be no combustion engines to power motors. These are just a few

Dousing flames with water is the most common way that firefighters remove heat from a fire.

THE LET-BURN POLICY

Many people believe that fires ruin forests. They are against setting deliberate fires and want all fires to be fought. But some people think that fires can help forests and believe in setting prescribed fires—fires used to burn off fuel on the forest floor in order to prevent huge wildfires from forming.

For a long time, most U.S. government agencies thought they should fight all fires in order to protect the forests. But by the 1960s, national fire research was looking at the benefits of fire. Today, some forest agencies try to completely put out fires. Others let fires burn, but try to carefully control them.

In 1972, the National Park Service adopted a "let-burn" policy, and the Forest Service came up with a similar plan. This policy means that fires are allowed to burn "naturally." The Park Service had discovered that fires help the forest keep its natural character. Also, if small, controlled fires clear the land, large fires do not grow even larger when they hit.

In Yellowstone National Park, administrators decided to let lightning-caused fires burn naturally. If a fire threatened people, historic sites, wildlife, or land outside the park, firefighters would stop it. A fire caused by humans would not be allowed to burn. Also, to help prevent big fires, the National Park Service would use fire to clear off dead trees and other dangerous forest fuels.

In the Yellowstone fires of 1988, all but one fire was thought to have been caused by lightning. But citizens wanted the fires put out. In the end, they believed that damage done to the park could have been prevented if firefighters had attacked the fires right away. Residents who feared for their businesses and homes were especially upset.

"In a dry year, they should have put these fires out," said Verlene Schmire, owner of a grocery store in West Yellowstone. "Our town and our businesses are going up in smoke. They've let a national treasure be destroyed."

But Yellowstone Superintendent Robert Barbee insisted that the fires had become destructive because of weather conditions, not park policy. According to Barbee, the fires had been good for the park. "Yellowstone is still the magnificent place it always has been; fires are a part of the life processes here, and the park will heal and regenerate its natural scars as it has countless times before. I'm excited about that process."

ways we have learned to use fire. But fire can change from a powerful tool into a deadly force if it is not managed properly. It is up to humankind to study the properties of fire and learn how to live with it safely.

Forest Fires

It is difficult to know just how far and wide a fire in the woods will burn—there are so many variables to consider, like the shape of the land and weather conditions. For this reason, scientists have begun to study the actual behavior of fire. Fire behavior refers to the way a fire develops. By learning more about the way fires start, scientists can help firefighters combat the flames.

There are two things scientists know affect fire behavior. One is ignition, which is the heating process that occurs at the beginning of combustion. The second is fire spread, which is

Opposite:
The effects of a fire in the wild depend on many factors, including the fuel available, weather conditions, and the contour of the land.

the way fire moves through fuels once ignited. The shape of the land (topography), weather conditions, and the nature of fuels available all affect how fire travels.

Land Like a Chimney

In North America, land is shaped in many different ways. There are flatlands, mountains, and hills. On flatlands, fire usually spreads out evenly in all directions, and travels much more quickly in one direction if the wind is blowing.

If a fire starts at the top of a hill, it will travel downward, but it does so very slowly. On a slope, fire travels upward fairly quickly. Fire moves even faster if it starts in a canyon or valley. The extreme slope of the land acts as a chimney, creating a draft that pulls the fire toward the top. For this reason, it is easy to get trapped at the top of a hill in a forest fire.

Fire in the Snow

Many different weather conditions affect fire spread, including precipitation, temperature, and humidity. A lot of rain and snow can cool a fire, so that the heat generated falls below the ignition point and the fire is smothered. However, if the fire is big enough and precipitation is light, the heat from the fire simply turns the snow or rain into vapor.

Humidity also helps slow down the heating process. If there is moisture in the air for a long period of time, the fuels a fire would feed on will contain some moisture.

In cold climates, wildfires cannot heat up as quickly as in warmer climates, making it more difficult for a fire to reach ignition point.

The charred remains of a forest slope smolder after a fire cleared the area in Washington.

Fuel Affects Fire

The nature of the fuels available contributes greatly to the spread of fire. Old, dry trees burn easily. Younger trees tend to be more moist, and take longer to ignite.

△ 17

If you've ever made a campfire, you already know that it is easier to start a fire with small, dry fuels, like kindling or twigs. They are placed at the bottom of the pile, and larger fuels, like logs, are placed at the top. There must also be some space between the firewood. If the fuel is packed too tightly, the fire cannot get enough oxygen to burn quickly. Loosely packed fuels that allow air to circulate around them promote fires most effectively.

Three Types of Fires

The ignition and fuel factors contribute to the classification of a fire as a ground fire, a surface fire, or a crown fire. In a ground fire, flames

A ground fire spreads across the floor of a forest in the Pacific Northwest. Ground fires often produce a great deal of smoke, but relatively little flame.

crawl along the forest floor, feeding on tightly packed leaves, pine needles, and moss. This kind of fire can produce a lot of smoke and very little flame. In a surface fire, flames find fuel in shrubs and grasses. The fire burns fast and gives off more heat than a ground fire. In a crown fire, the flames from a surface fire find their way to the tops of trees, up what is called a fire ladder. Trees that have dead, dry branches provide this ladder for the flames.

A crown fire is extremely dangerous. Flames can leap across tree tops, traveling quickly. In the worst of these fires, called either firestorms or blowups, tornado-like currents are created. Trees snap and fly off into a hot swirl. Large pieces of burning wood, known as firebrands, are thrown ahead of the fire and thick, black smoke completely darkens the sky.

Blowups have caused some of the worst disasters in history. Scientists have estimated that these fires burn with the intensity of an atomic bomb exploding every two minutes. Over a century ago, one of these terrifying fires swept through Wisconsin.

Peshtigo, Wisconsin: 1871

Peshtigo, Wisconsin is a town surrounded by forest, and it was experiencing a dry spell. Small fires had been popping up at various

The Peshtigo fire of 1871 killed an estimated 800 people and destroyed over 1 million acres (405,000 hectares) of land.

locations in the woods, and all the smoke from these fires caused people's eyes to water. One resident noted, "Unless we have rain soon, a conflagration [a fire too big to be put out with water] may destroy this town."

Many people had been fighting the small fires and taking measures to prevent greater ones. Ditches that acted as fire lines were dug around mills so that fires could not cross over.

But on October 8, 1871, a wind stirred up black clouds of soot, which brought on complete darkness, and a low roar was heard. The sound grew louder, and trees fell to the ground.

Flashes from firebrands lit the darkened sky. The powerful wind traveled up to 80 miles (129 kilometers) per hour and lifted roofs off houses. Many who survived what came next spoke of "fire balloons" exploding above ground. These were probably bubbles of gases from the actual fire, ignited by the heat.

The roaring noise increased, sounding like the pounding of heavy freight trains. One veteran from the Civil War thought he was back in battle again, facing the big artillery of the Confederate Army. Those who thought that the Day of Judgment had come fell to the ground and simply gave up.

The "fire balloons" dropped from the sky, and swallowed up the land. Hundreds of people who ran to a stream for protection were trampled by terrified cattle. Many others who hid in root cellars, wells, and stone buildings died from asphyxiation (lack of oxygen) or they were burned alive. Forty people died when a boardinghouse exploded into flames. Another 150 people ran to a marshy area on the bank of the river and held on to the wet ground. Luckily, they survived.

Within an hour, the town of Peshtigo was in ashes. As the fire raged on, it destroyed several other towns and over 1 million acres (405,000 hectares) of land. It was estimated that more than 800 people died. At the time, it was the worst forest fire disaster ever in the United States.

The town of Peshtigo was rebuilt, but it took many more years and a whole wave of deadly fires to finally convince people to take more effective preventive measures against fire.

Rocky Mountains: 1910

On August 20, 1910, fires that had been raging across the Rocky Mountains grew into a fierce blowup. Firefighters knew they faced a battle that could not be won. Many men became hysterical, and some, afraid of burning to death, took their own lives. In one famous incident, a foreman saved almost all his crew.

He was Edward Pulaski, a ranger (a person who protects a natural reserve from fire or other destructive forces) who had been a miner in the region for twenty-five years. When Pulaski felt the strong wind and heard the great roar of the blowup, he knew it was time to evacuate. He rounded up his men, 45 in all, and started them toward the town of Wallace, Idaho. But the path was blocked by fire. Pulaski then led his crew to a nearby mine shaft. One man was hit and crushed by a falling tree.

The crew fled into the War Eagle mine. At the back of the mine, Pulaski instructed the men to douse themselves with water trickling from a spring. Pulaski himself went to the front of the mine to make sure the fire did not come close enough to destroy the mine timbers. If this happened before he could alert the men, the entrance would be sealed off. The heat, smoke, and gases that filled the cave were so unbearable that all the men, including Pulaski, soon lost consciousness.

Luckily, all but 5 of the men in the cave survived. To firefighters everywhere, Edward Pulaski was a real hero.

The 1910 blowup changed the way America would fight fires in future years. The Rocky Mountain fires convinced Gifford Pinchot, chief of the Forest Service, that all fires should be fought. That year, the Forest Service became responsible for fighting the nation's forest fires, and under Pinchot's leadership, it developed methods of fighting fires. Roads and trails were built to make the forests easy for firefighters to get to. Observation towers were built, and telephone lines were put up to link them.

By 1935, after the Forest Service discovered that aggressive firefighting kept small fires from getting out of hand, it came up with what is known as the "10 A.M. Policy." In this plan, all fires would have to be put out by 10 A.M. the following day, before the hottest and driest part of the day could make the fire bigger and more dangerous. But blowups continued to occur, and the Forest Service began to experiment with setting fires in order to burn off fuel on forest floors. These experiments showed that fire could help a forest.

New Ontario, Canada: 1916

A heat wave in the summer of 1916 made the land in New Ontario, Canada, extremely dry. By July, the area had gone without rain for two months. Although Matheson, Iroquois Falls, and Cochrane counties were dry, no one seemed concerned about fire. Settlers were burning off their property (to inexpensively clear their land for farming), woodcutters were burning brush, and railway workers were clearing scrub near the tracks.

No one knows how "the big fire" started, but when it happened, on July 29, six communities felt the worst of its fury.

The fire took no lives in Matheson. In the area outside the community, however, families suffocated in their root cellars and wells. Some were burned as they tried to outrun a wall of fire that was 40 miles (64 kilometers) wide.

At Iroquois Falls, 8 people died. The fire first showed itself as a rolling mass of black clouds. According to resident Isabelle Scott, "The sun looked like a huge ball of blood in the sky." The whole place darkened and fell silent. Then the fire hit town.

Cochrane had experienced bad fires before. After a fire in 1911, it put in a new water system that could pump from lakes to the north and south. When the fire hit in 1916, the Cochrane volunteer fire department drew water from the lakes. But the heat from the fire was so intense that the water turned to steam in the hoses.

By the evening of July 30, the fire had begun to die out and a heavy rain put it out completely. Cochrane's business district was in ruins. Matheson, Iroquois Falls, and several other small towns were devastated. About 50,000 acres (20,235 hectares) were burned. According to the official record, 223 people died. This number still stands as the largest death toll from a Canadian forest fire in the twentieth century.

The Canadian Forestry Association urged New Ontario to increase its number of rangers and to better control people who tried to clear their land with fire.

Yellowstone National Park: 1988

In 1988, one of the largest battles against fire ever took place in Yellowstone National Park. The park is situated in the northwest corner of Wyoming and includes smaller pieces of Montana to the north and Idaho to the southwest.

A bison flees Yellowstone during one of the worst forest fires in American history.

More than 9,000 firefighters took to the forest. They used hand tools, bulldozers, fire trucks, airplanes, helicopters, and other equipment. In total, about $120 million was spent to fight the Yellowstone blaze.

The weather in the previous few winters had been very dry. Even though it had rained during the summers, it was not enough to make up for the lack of winter precipitation.

In the summer of 1988, a drought set in. Not since 1886 (when a fire in Yellowstone forest prompted the beginning of the U.S. government's involvement with fighting forest fires) had it ever been so dry in Yellowstone. Brush fires throughout the region and strong winds helped to nearly double the number of fires that normally occurred in the area. The wind drove fires leaping across the land. Fires even jumped the Grand Canyon of the Yellowstone River, which is 0.5 miles (0.8 kilometers) wide at its narrowest section.

Throughout the summer, news programs showed flames that were 200 feet (61 meters) high, clouds of black smoke, glowing orange skies, and exhausted firefighters black with soot. Many people were afraid that the park would be completely ruined. In fact, 995,000 acres (403,000 hectares), almost half of the park, had been burned.

Severe drought created the extremely dry conditions that fostered the Yellowstone fire in 1988.

In the end, Yellowstone was not lost. At the time of the fire, 80 percent of the forest was lodgepole pine trees that were over 100 years old. These trees actually require heat for their cones to open and release seeds. Right after the fire swept through Yellowstone, it was found that the lodgepole cones were releasing seeds. Many other kinds of plants also began to grow back after the fire.

Although a number of animals escaped the fire and survived, investigators found 250 elk, 12 moose, 36 mule deer, 4 bison, and 6 black

△ **27**

Natural fires often have some positive effects on the environment. During the months and years following the Yellowstone fire, vegetation was renewed, providing a richer and more varied food supply for the area's wildlife.

bears dead in the forest. Nearly all of them died of asphyxiation. Animals that survived returned to Yellowstone almost immediately to enjoy the benefits of the fire. Squirrels and birds came back to eat the cone seeds that had dropped to the ground. Bears and coyotes returned to consume animals that died during the fire.

Environmental researchers have found that three times as many plants and animals live in a forest after a fire than were there before the fire happened. In Yellowstone, during the spring of 1989, the vegetation actually grew more plentiful and many animals came to feed there.

Oakland, California: 1991

In California, many urban neighborhoods situated close to forest areas are vulnerable to fire.

Karen Terrill, spokeswoman for the state's Department of Forestry and Fire Prevention, worries because so many homes have been built in heavily wooded areas throughout the state of California.

"Sixty-one percent of California is covered with wildlands," says Terrill. "Fire is just part of California's ecological makeup. California was built to burn."

In October 1991, a terrible urban forest fire raged through Oakland, California. The area had suffered five years of drought and although the summer of 1991 had been relatively cool, the month of October was hot. On Saturday, October 19, a brush fire in the Oakland Hills was sighted. Firefighters contained it, but did not fully extinguish it.

Aided by strong winds that reached 36 miles (58 kilometers) per hour, the brush fire erupted into a blaze on Sunday that roared through the crowns of eucalyptus trees. These trees, imported from Australia in 1856, are very oily and highly flammable. They tend to explode rather than burn.

The dry trees and brush nearby were quickly consumed. Then the fire was blown to the southeast through urban areas. Houses, some covered with cedar shingles, became fuel for the fire.

As burning cedar shingles were torn loose and carried by the wind to other areas, the fire spread very quickly. Flames whipped through neighborhoods, and people began to flee. One man, Tom Skelly, said he was watching a football game at about 11:30 A.M. on Sunday, when he heard a car horn honking outside. Suddenly a neighbor ran in with the news.

Skelly said he and his wife, Martha, could see a curtain of red beating its way up the parched brush. They grabbed their two cats and jumped in their car, fleeing their home of twenty-five years. As they drove away, Martha rolled down her car window, and the flames seared her clothes and burned the seat cover. However, the couple escaped unharmed.

Not everyone was as lucky. The fire killed 25 people and destroyed more than 3,000 homes.

Fire trucks crowd the scene in an Oakland, California, neighborhood during the fire of 1991.

The Oakland firestorm was described as one in which nearly everything went wrong. The land was dry, the humidity was low, and the wind was strong. Also, firefighters were hampered by an old communication system and a lack of water pressure at critical times.

"Prevention is the key," said Forestry Director Richard Wilson. "We have greater technological capacity to fight these fires, but in a contest with nature, nature usually wins." Wilson suggested that future housing developments in wooded areas have a fire plan, that brush be cleared away from houses, and evacuation routes be set in advance. "Without prevention," Wilson said, "disasters are waiting to happen."

California Firestorm: 1993

Only a couple of years after the Oakland disaster, another California firestorm took its toll. Starting on October 27, 1993, a series of fires swept through the hills of southern California. In fact, 26 firestorms eventually resulted in 3 deaths and destroyed about 1,000 homes. The fires from Ventura county ranged to the Mexican border, burning more than 140,000 acres (57,000 hectares) and 660 houses. President Clinton declared Los Angeles, Orange, Riverside, San Diego, and Ventura counties disaster areas, making them eligible for federal assistance.

△ **31**

As in Oakland, conditions were perfect for such destruction. The firestorms were aided by drought, large amounts of brush, high temperatures, low humidity, and Santa Ana winds. The Santa Ana winds are strong, dry, hot winds that sweep down from mountain sides from the north, northeast, or east in southern California. As cool air passes over the mountains, it compresses, gains heat, and then loses humidity. The Santa Ana winds can blow at 100 miles (161 kilometers) per hour.

In addition to natural conditions being right for fire, authorities suspected that a number of fires were caused by people. The Altadena fire, in Los Angeles county, was reportedly started by a homeless man trying to keep warm.

"It's likely that many of the fires were human-caused. Whether they were arson or not, we don't know. It can be even a hot tailpipe that sparks a fire," said Lisa Boyd, spokeswoman for the California Department of Forestry and Fire Protection.

More than 7,000 firefighters battled the firestorms. Said one exhausted firefighter, Robert Reysden, "I haven't seen a bed for days. I've been trying to sleep on top of the engine."

Along with exhaustion came a feeling of awe, for the fires were like none ever seen by most firefighters and residents. Firestorm '93, as

Firestorms swept through southern California in 1993. The flames raged for days in many residential neighborhoods. Here, a Malibu resident stands on the front steps of what used to be her mother's home.

the devastating brush fires were being called, inspired a fearful respect in all who encountered the flames.

"You felt hopeless," said firefighter Jerry Thompson. "Everyone's dream was going up in flames and there was nothing you could do."

City Fires

Throughout history, fire has destroyed whole cities. From its very beginning, the United States was plagued by such fires. In December 1607, a fire swept through Jamestown, Virginia. Many of the settlers died that winter because without shelter they were exposed to the cold climate. But the settlement was rebuilt and became the capital of the Virginia colony.

As towns grew larger, fires became an increasingly serious problem because more fuel (in the form of wooden buildings) was available to feed the flames.

Opposite:
The great Chicago fire of 1871 engulfed the city after months of drought created dangerously dry conditions.

Some towns were wiped out by fires traveling from forests or prairies, while others were damaged by fires that started in town from a variety of causes.

Chicago, Illinois: 1871

In 1871, Chicago had a population of 334,000. Some of its buildings were made of iron and stone, but thousands were built of wood. The streets and sidewalks were also wooden.

As in Peshtigo, Wisconsin, Chicago was suffering from a drought. There had already been a number of small fires when a large fire broke out on Saturday night, October 7, 1871. Throughout the night, 90 firefighters—almost half of the city's fire department—battled the flames. By morning, 20 acres (8 hectares) of Chicago's West Side had burned and 30 firefighters were injured.

Then, on Sunday evening, another fire was spotted in a barn owned by Kate and Patrick O'Leary. According to the popularly held legend, a cow had gotten angry at Mrs. O'Leary for milking it so late at night, and it kicked over a kerosene lantern. The fire spread north and northeast, carried by the wind. Thirty buildings were in flames before firefighters arrived.

The heat from the fire was so intense that limestone buildings began to melt. Bodies were

completely consumed in the fire, bone and all. Whirlwinds, created by the heat, carried burning embers across the city, starting other fires. Soon the fire had moved to the south. About 76,000 citizens were in the street, fleeing their homes in search of safety.

When the fire reached the waterworks the next morning, the city's pumps were ruined, and there was no way to fight the fire. Only a heavy rain could save Chicago. On Monday night, at around 11 P.M., the rain came. By 3:00 A.M. on Tuesday, the fire had finally gone out. At least 300 people had died in the flames, and a third of the city had been destroyed.

The Chicago fire of 1871 left many buildings and homes in ashen ruins.

△ 37

San Francisco, California: 1906

During the late 1800s and early 1900s, many cities were taking measures against fire, but no city could really prepare for an earthquake. Even so, San Franciscans can look back to 1906 and see that the city lost much by not heeding the warning of one of its fire chiefs.

Officials at City Hall had been told by Fire Chief Dennis T. Sullivan that San Francisco would burn if a big earthquake hit. On the morning of April 18, this prediction came true. The San Andreas fault, which runs through much of California, shifted under San Francisco.

People were awakened in their beds, which were moving about their rooms. Buildings were crashing, windows were shattering, and screams could be heard throughout the city.

When people came out into the streets, they watched the dust settle long enough to find that danger still lay ahead. The earthquake had knocked over lanterns, candles, and stoves. It had buckled streets, cracked gas and water lines, and had sent live electrical lines flying. Everywhere, there was fire.

San Francisco was 90 percent wood, and it was set among steep hills. With water mains damaged, communication disrupted, and a stiff wind blowing, the fire department had a major challenge ahead.

SALVAGE BAGS AND STREET FIGHTS

Before the first volunteer fire departments were organized, groups of people in a city or town came together at a fire and tried to "water it down" and save as many valuables as possible in what were called salvage bags. These groups were known as fire societies.

Then, in 1736, after seeing several big fires in Boston and Philadelphia, Benjamin Franklin organized America's first volunteer fire department, called the Union Fire Company, in Philadelphia. More fire companies were soon formed. The volunteers provided their own equipment, including buckets, ladders, and salvage bags.

At a fire, the chief of each company would set up a bucket brigade, which was made up of crews of firefighters who handed buckets of water down a line. The water was thrown on the fire by the person closest to it at the end of the line. Volunteers would try very hard to save as many valuables as possible in their salvage bags.

Benjamin Franklin recognized the need for fire insurance. People could pay to have his company insure their losses. Also, Franklin's company was one of the first to use fire marks—lead molded symbols put outside houses, telling volunteer firefighters which insurance company was responsible for repaying losses. Today, these fire marks can be found on some buildings from the colonial era.

As more fire companies formed across the nation, they became very competitive. In San Francisco, each company raised money to build its own station house and to buy all of its equipment and uniforms. Citizens out at the sound of an alarm to watch the favorite companies race for a fire. They rooted them on as they would a sports team.

In 1865, competition came to a head. The Monumental Six and Social Three companies took on the Knickerbocker Five company in a bloody hand-to-hand battle in the streets of San Francisco. They fought each other with fire tools, knives, cobblestones, and guns. People were so alarmed by the violence that the city finally decided to create one big firefighting company and call it the San Francisco Fire Department.

Most of the fire protection services in the United States today are provided by local governments. Communities fund their own fire departments, which consist of fire stations, equipment, and personnel. However, like in colonial times, people still volunteer to fight fires all across America.

A colonial fire pump with volunteers.

Troops walk down Market Street after the San Francisco earthquake of 1906.

Running 3 miles (5 kilometers) wide, the fire moved across the city destroying buildings. The fire department tried using dynamite on some buildings, hoping to use the rubble as a fire line. This tactic did not work. The fire actually burned through the shattered buildings more easily. Finally, after three full days, the wind changed and pushed the fire back toward the burned out part of the city, where it was stopped from lack of fuel.

The San Francisco fire and earthquake of 1906 caused horrible damage. According to some reports, an estimated 700 people died. Approximately 350 people were missing, possibly consumed by the extreme heat of the fire. And about 25,000 buildings had been destroyed. Five square miles (13 square kilometers) of the city lay in ruins, and 300,000 people were without homes. City Hall, a new building that had taken almost thirty years and $8 million dollars to build, crumbled to the ground in the early hours of this catastrophe.

The Triangle Shirtwaist Factory Fire, New York City: 1911

It was a Saturday, on March 25, 1911. More than 600 employees labored in the Triangle Shirtwaist Company, in New York City, sewing materials into blouses.

Suddenly, someone on the eighth floor spotted a fire in a rag bin. A few people tried to put it out with water, but the flames had spread to the tables where the cloth lay. Within a very short time, the eighth floor was full of flames. Workers began racing for the only two exits off the floor. One door had been bolted shut by

Firefighters battle the inferno at the Triangle Shirtwaist Factory in New York City, 1911.

managers to keep workers from sneaking out for a break. The other door could only be approached through a narrow passageway, and the two elevators in the building held about twelve people at a time. Even so, most of the people on the eighth floor managed to get out of the building.

One of those who escaped was Celia Saltz. "All I could think," she said later, "was that I must run to the door. I didn't know there was a fire escape. I even forgot that I had a younger sister working with me."

"The door to the staircase wouldn't open." Celia said. "We pushed to the passenger elevators. Everybody was pushing and screaming. When the car stopped at our floor I was pushed into it by the crowd. I began to scream for my sister. I had lost her. I had lost my sister."

Celia fainted in the elevator car. When she came to, she was lying down on the floor in a building across the street. Her sister Minnie was bending over her.

On the ninth floor, however, workers were not so lucky. After the flames from below came in through windows and set fabric on fire, the whole floor was ablaze. About 300 workers tried to escape. But, as on the eighth floor, one door was locked, and a narrow passageway slowed down their escape.

Desperate for safety from the fire, more than 30 women jumped into the elevator shaft. Many of them were crushed. Others tried to use the fire escape, but the heat from the fire had softened the metal, causing it to twist away from the building. The women were thrown into a courtyard far below. Another 60 women went out on the window ledges to escape the fire, but the flames caught up with them. Then, to the horror of the people on the street below, these women jumped to their death.

Within minutes, firefighters had arrived on the scene, but aerial ladders could reach only up to the sixth floor, and water pumps only to the seventh. The people on the ninth floor were doomed.

The ruins of a factory floor lie in a charred heap at the Triangle Shirtwaist Factory.

The fire was brought under control within eighteen minutes. But 146 people were dead or dying. Another 70 were seriously injured.

Besides the doors to one stairway having been locked, there were other fire-safety problems. There was no sprinkler system in the building, and a third staircase required by law had never been constructed. Following this tragedy, the state of New York formed the Factory Investigating Commission on June 30, 1911.

Boston, Massachusetts: 1942

It was November 28, 1942, and the United States was fighting in World War II. Still, that night, thousands went out to have a little fun.

The Cocoanut Grove, a famous dance hall in Boston, was crowded. At least 1,000 people were there. Decorations made the place look

The burnt exterior of the Cocoanut Grove dance hall in Boston, Massachusetts, provided an eerie reminder of the tragedy that took place inside.

like a tropical paradise, filled with palm trees and bamboo chairs. The dance hall even had a ceiling lined with blue satin.

Everything seemed to be going as usual. People were dancing and talking—it was nice to get away from the seriousness of war. Then a fire broke out above a palm tree, and began eating through the blue satin sky. Waiters tried to put it out with water, but the fire continued to burn.

At first the guests stood by quietly, in awe of the spreading fire. Then, they must have realized they were in danger—the fire was growing out of control. Suddenly, it seemed, 200 people in the downstairs room were running for one exit. It was a narrow stairway leading to the main floor. But the flames ran faster than the people, reaching the top of the stairs and spreading through that next floor.

This wave of flame was followed by thick, black smoke. It was dark and the whole main floor was filled with a choking, sooty cloud. Most of the exits were either locked or jammed. Two others opened inward. People raced to these doors, creating a human wall against which the doors could not open. Within minutes, 491 people were dead or mortally injured, and hundreds needed medical care. Only 100 people escaped without physical harm.

Atlanta, Georgia: 1946

Around the turn of the century, some builders started calling their new structures "fireproof." People began to believe that fire had been conquered. These buildings had thick walls and floors made of nonflammable material. Usually, they had fire escapes, either on the outside or inside. But events would prove that there is no such thing as a fireproof building.

Standing fifteen stories high and built with both brick and cement, the great Winecoff Hotel in Atlanta, Georgia, was considered "fireproof." However, it had no fire escapes and no sprinkler system. W. F. Winecoff, the builder, was confident that his building was safe. He even lived in the hotel until the day he died. That day was December 7, 1946, the day the hotel caught fire.

According to one story, a match was carelessly dropped onto a mattress stored on the third floor. From there, wooden baseboards, doors, carpeting, dressers, beds, and painted walls caught fire. The elevators stopped working, and the stairway became an alley for the flames. Most of the guests were trapped, cut off from any hope of safety or rescue.

When firefighters arrived, just seconds after the alarm sounded, they saw people hanging out of the windows. Some had knotted sheets

Owner and builder W. F. Winecoff believed his Atlanta hotel was "fireproof" until it went up in flames in December 1946.

together and had started climbing down, only to find that their makeshift ropes did not reach the ground. The heat or smoke had overtaken some of the guests. Another 25 jumped to their deaths. One of those who jumped collided with a firefighter carrying a woman down a ladder. All 3 died in a violent crash below.

△ 47

Before the fire was brought under control, 119 people had lost their lives. One was W. F. Winecoff. He died in his own hotel in the worst hotel fire in American history.

Mexico City, Mexico: 1988

Carelessness and neglect are often the cause of fire, but corruption may also play a role. In Mexico City, Mexico, just two weeks before Christmas in 1988, the illegal sale of fireworks, and the lack of action by officials to prevent those sales, caused a very deadly fire.

Selling fireworks to the general public was barred in Mexico, but people could still easily buy them.

On December 11, in a crowded market on Corona Street, shoppers were very busy buying food, presents, and fireworks to celebrate the upcoming holiday.

Suddenly, a blast occurred, setting off a chain reaction of explosions that ripped like machine-gun fire through other stalls where vendors had been selling skyrockets and Roman candles. Flames quickly spread throughout the market, setting five buildings on fire. Many people were trapped inside these buildings and died.

"People were running out of the market and screaming," said Oscar Cordero, a vendor who had been selling electronic goods.

At least 80 people were injured, and 52 perished, including 12 children.

Although the illegal sale of fireworks had gone on for years, recognized by some as part of Mexican culture, many people were angry.

"It was a time bomb," said Elizabeth Diaz, a member of the union of market vendors. "There's hundreds of people who come here to sell them [illegal fireworks]. They have for years. Why didn't the authorities come?"

According to one municipal leader, named Everado Gamiz Fernandez, inspections in the market were not very frequent. "There aren't enough resources to watch here every day and night," he stated.

In America, many states have outlawed fireworks, but some products, such as cherry bombs, M-80s, silver salutes, and M-100s, are sold illegally. Although all fireworks are hazardous, illegal products pose extra dangers. They are usually very powerful and made without the same quality control standards of legal products.

People die from both fireworks injuries and from fires started by fireworks. In the same year as the Mexico City fire, about 10,200 people with injuries from fireworks reported to U.S. emergency rooms. Physicians and firefighters strongly suggest that people leave fireworks to professionals.

C H A P T E R

Preventing and Fighting Fires

Fire is dangerous, and fighting it is a dangerous profession. In 1992, when U.S. fire departments responded to almost two million calls, 74 firefighters died in the line of duty.

Whether in a forest or a city, firefighters treat their job as a battle and act as an army. First and foremost, they require training and the proper equipment. When they go into action, they go in with a plan, as organized units. Firefighters maintain communication and respect a strict chain of command, starting with a fire chief or commander. Using disciplined and

Opposite:
A helicopter drops fire retardants on a California wildfire.

Training to be a firefighter is a long, grueling task. Here, a team of trainees learn how to work in unison while battling a blaze.

proven strategies for attacking fires allows firefighters to operate most effectively, saving lives and property.

Firefighters must pass a number of exams. If accepted into a fire department, they undergo tough training programs, learning how to handle equipment like hoses, ladders, and power tools. They learn about different smoke and fire situations. They study the chemistry of fire, hazards of natural gas and electricity, how to handle toxins, and first-aid techniques. Finally, they drill repeatedly on procedures and fire-fighting techniques, so that they will be prepared whenever an alarm comes in.

Equipment and Technology

For the past sixty years, strict building codes and fire-resistant materials have been used in the construction of most buildings across North America, in an attempt to reduce the chances of a structure being burned to ashes in a matter of minutes.

Fire towers have given people a better view for sighting forest fires. Tower operators can now communicate by phone and map fires on a big compass-like device, called the Osbourn Firefinder. Fire spotters in airplanes can inspect large, often wild, areas easily.

Satellites are also used to map fires. Infrared images are transmitted from satellites to spotter planes, where a map showing the hot areas of a fire is created.

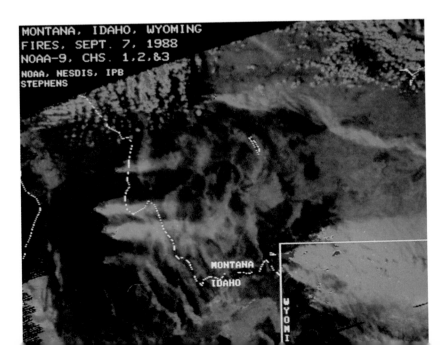

MONTANA, IDAHO, WYOMING FIRES, SEPT. 7, 1988 NOAA-9, CHS. 1,2,&3
NOAA, NESDIS, IPB STEPHENS

A satellite photo tracks the progress of the Yellowstone fire in 1988. The red spots show the active Yellowstone fires.

Computers also help bring information together quickly. Weather stations called *RAWS* (remote automated weather stations) sense wind speed and direction, air humidity, temperature, and the conditions of soil, brush, and timber. This data is relayed to satellites and then to computers at a control center, called the Interagency Fire Center in Boise, Idaho. The control center works to coordinate firefighting efforts in a forest fire emergency.

Also, more than thirty sensors mounted on poles across the western United States send messages to the control center computers, telling them where lightning is striking.

According to Ken Reninger, a U.S. Bureau of Land Management official, this technology has improved forest fire detection and suppression. "Reacting in the past was almost always a case of gut feeling, and we often paid a price. We used to fly planes around everywhere just looking for a fire. It was like jumping in a taxi and saying 'Take me someplace.' Now we can go directly to where the lightning hit."

Warriors of the Woods

When there is a fire in the forest, line crews take to the woods. They are the first wave of defense, using hand tools and bulldozers to make fire lines. When the commander arrives, he or she examines the fire conditions—fuel that is still available, slopes that the fire might race up, the weather, and natural fire lines like roads and rivers that might help stop the fire.

When the forest is an especially rugged one, helitack teams are brought in by helicopter, and smoke jumpers come in cargo planes and parachute down to the fire. These teams are usually coordinated by the rangers in the district where the fire is taking place.

When fires are extremely threatening, hotshot crews are sent in. There are about a dozen of these hotshot crews throughout the United States. They consist of well-trained firefighters who fly all over the country responding to urgent calls.

To back up all of these forces, aerial bombers may be called in to drop water. Tanker planes can carry up to 3,000 gallons (11,370 liters) of water and fire retardants. They drop their load over the fire, covering areas that are otherwise unreachable.

Aerial bombers can be valuable resources for fighting exceptionally hard-to-control fires.

An Ounce of Prevention

Sometimes the only positive result of a fire is a lesson about future safety and fire awareness.

Today, there is a recognized need for better fire safety education, so that people can learn how to prevent fires or how to escape from them if they should occur. Fire-safety messages are often aired on television. In many countries where safety messages and ads are used, there is a relatively low fire rate. Where forest fires are concerned, Smokey the Bear is probably the most popular figure reminding people to be careful with matches in the forest.

In response to the 1871 fire, one of the most famous fires in American history, a new fire code was created for the city of Chicago. All public doors would open outwards and would have "panic bars" so that people could push through even more easily in the event of an emergency. Also, buildings would have to have automatic sprinkler systems. Other cities in the United States and around the world learned from this costly fire and adopted Chicago's codes.

In all places, especially in their homes, people need to take responsibility for their own safety and that of their families. In 1992, 78 percent of all fire deaths occurred in the home. A great majority of these fires could have been prevented or stopped early if a few precautions

SMOKEY THE BEAR

The birth of Smokey the Bear goes back to World War II, when the Forest Service began a campaign promoting fire prevention. After the southern California coast was shelled by a Japanese submarine in 1942, U.S. government officials realized how important timber was to the war effort. The enemy could really hamper the United States and its allies by causing fires. The government decided it needed to encourage the general public to help in fighting forest fires. The Forest Service then organized the Cooperative Forest Fire Prevention Program (CFFP).

Young fans visit with Smokey the Bear.

To get its message to Americans, the CFFP contacted the Wartime Advertising Council for help in coming up with a campaign. Early posters used wartime slogans. Then, in 1944, Walt Disney's character Bambi was used on prevention posters. After that, the Forest Service and the Wartime Advertising Council wanted to use a bear to represent forest fire prevention.

The bear was named after "Smokey" Joe Martin, Assistant Chief of the New York City Fire Department from 1919 to 1930. A radio newscaster named Jackson Weaver provided the bear's voice. With the slogan "Only you can prevent forest fires," Smokey reminded people to be careful of fire. Smokey the Bear's message on posters, in newspapers, and on the radio captured people's attention, and forest fires decreased in the United States.

In 1950, Smokey became a living symbol. In a fire in the Lincoln National Forest in New Mexico, a badly burned bear cub was found. Firefighters took the bear to a ranger station where he received special care. The rangers called him Smokey, after the famous poster bear. When Smokey was sent to the National Zoological Park in Washington, D.C., he became the symbol of forest fire prevention. Although he died in 1976, other bears have kept the symbol alive.

had been taken. The easiest—and perhaps most important—precaution to take is to install smoke detectors. Most detectors can be purchased for under $20, a small price to pay for something that can save the lives of an entire

Smoke detectors are just one of the many simple and inexpensive ways to help protect a building from the threat of fire.

family. In addition to installing smoke detectors, families should equip their homes with fire extinguishers.

What to Do in Case of a Fire

In addition to equipping their homes, families should make an escape plan. Such a plan should identify two ways to get out of every room in the house. If one path is blocked by fire, another escape route may be necessary.

Families should also practice their escape plans. Because fear, darkness, and confusion usually hinder attempts to get out of a burning building, it is recommended that families practice their escape plans in the dark.

As part of an escape plan, a family should choose a place to meet outside, so that it will be known immediately how many people are still in the house or that everyone is out.

When fire does occur, people inside the house should test every door for heat before opening it. If heat is felt in the crack between the door and the door frame, on the knob, or door, the alternate escape route should be used.

If smoke blocks the only path out of a burning house, crawl out. Smoke contains deadly gases and is hot. It rises toward the ceiling, leaving the air near the floor less harmful.

If your clothes catch on fire, it is best to follow the "stop, drop, and roll" routine. Don't run, but stop, drop to the ground and cover your face, then roll over and over to smother the flames.

People should get out quickly and stay out of a burning building. No one should ever go back into a burning house for any reason. If people do get trapped in a fire, the best thing for them to do is to close the doors against the fire and stuff the cracks around the doors to keep out smoke. If a phone is in the room, they should call the fire department. They should also try getting the attention of people on the outside.

With any fire, there can be a price to pay in both loss of life and loss of property. But, the sooner fires are detected, the better. When fires are still small they are easier to put out and usually have done less damage.

Of course, the best way to stop fires is to simply keep them from starting in the first place, when at all possible.

Glossary

arson The criminal act of setting fire to property.

asphyxiation Death or unconsciousness caused by lack of oxygen.

blowup A firestorm.

combustion A chemical process that produces heat and light.

crown fire A fire that travels quickly through the tops, or crowns, of trees.

fire A chemical reaction in which carbon or other compounds combine with oxygen, releasing heat and gases that ignite, producing flames and smoke.

fire line A line, or path, cleared of fuels by firefighters so that an advancing forest fire will have nothing to feed upon and will stop burning. In the city, a border at the site of a fire beyond which only firefighters may cross.

fire spread The way fire moves through fuels.

firestorm A big crown fire, often called a blowup, generating its own strong, high winds that carry it along.

fire triangle A symbol used to represent the three things needed for a fire to burn: heat, oxygen, and fuel.

ground fire A fire that crawls along the forest floor consuming packed leaves and needles.

helitack team A team of forest-firefighters who come in by helicopter.

ignition The heating process of a fuel at the start of a fire.

smoke jumper team A crew of firefighters who parachute from cargo planes to fires that are hard to reach.

surface fire A fire that feeds on branches hanging from trees and on shrubs and grasses.

wildfire An uncontrolled fire.

wildland Land that is not cleared and prepared for crops.

Further Reading

Burks, John. *Working Fire.* San Francisco: Chronicle Books, 1985.

Kent, Zachary. *The Story of the Triangle Factory Fire.* Chicago: Childrens Press, 1989.

Lauber, Patricia. *Summer of Fire: Yellowstone 1988.* New York: Orchard Books, 1991.

Lee, Mary P. and Lee, Richard S. *Careers in Firefighting.* New York: Rosen Publishing, 1993.

Smith, Dennis. *Dennis Smith's History of Firefighting in America: 300 Years of Courage.* New York: Dial Press, 1978.

Vogt, Gregory. *Forests on Fire: The Fight to Save Our Trees.* New York: Franklin Watts, 1990.

HAVE YOU EVER FACED A DISASTER?

If you have ever had to be brave enough to face a fire, you probably have a few exciting stories to tell! Twenty-First Century Books invites you to write us a letter and share your experiences. The letter can describe any aspect of your true story—how you felt during the disaster; what happened to you, your family, or other people in your area; or how the disaster changed your life. Please send your letter to Disaster Editor, TFCB, 115 West 18th Street, New York, NY 10011. We look forward to hearing from you!

Source Notes

Begley, Sharon. "Fighting Fires Bit by Byte." *Newsweek,* August 1989.

Forest Service. *Centennial Mini-Histories of the Forest Service.* 1992.

_____. *Fire Management Notes.* 1992-1993.

_____. *Highlights in the History of Forest Conservation.* 1976.

_____. *History Line.* 1993.

Nordwall, Bruce D. "Airborne Surveillance Will Give Forest Service Real Time Fire Maps." *Aviation Week and Space Technology,* May 29, 1989.

Pyne, Stephen J. *Fire in America.* Princeton: Princeton University Press, 1982.

Schullery, Paul. "After the Fires." *National Parks,* November 1989.

Smith, Dennis. *Dennis Smith's History of Firefighting in America.* New York: Dial Press, 1978.

Stein, Leon. *The Triangle Fire.* New York: Lippincott, 1962.

Trooper, Tom. "The Dragon Slayers." *Mother Earth News,* 1987.

Vogt, Gregory. *Forests on Fire.* New York: Franklin Watts, 1990.

Wasserman, Stuart. "Of Fire and Forests." *Sierra,* May 1988.

Wells, Robert W. *Fire at Peshtigo.* Englewood Cliffs, NJ: Prentice-Hall, 1990.

Index

Acknowledgements and Photo Credits

Cover: ©Mike Brown/Gamma-Liaison; p. 4: ©Bruce S. de Lis/Gamma-Liaison; pp. 6, 37, 43, 44, 47: UPI/Bettmann; p. 7: UPI/Bettmann Newsphotos; p. 9: Gamma-Liaison; p. 12: K. Argue/Liaison; pp. 14, 50: Al Golub/Liaison USA; p. 17: Yuen-Gi Lee/USDA Forest Service; p. 18: USDA Forest Service; pp. 20, 39, 40, 42: The Bettmann Archive; pp. 25, 27, 28: National Park Service; p. 30: Lysaght/Liaison USA; p. 33: Reuters/Bettmann; p. 34: ©Blackbirch Press, Inc.; p. 52: ©Paul S. Howell/Liaison International; p. 53: The National Oceanic and Atmospheric Administration; p. 55: Ponopresse/Gamma-Liaison; p. 57: Forest History Society, Inc.; p. 58: BRK Electronics, Inc.